How to Beat the High Cost of Health Care

How to Beat the High Cost of Health Care

✦

the "Total Benefits" Strategy

Thomas J. Quigley,
Edward A. Lyon, J.D.

with Jennifer L. Nevin,
Christy A. Quigley

iUniverse, Inc.
New York Lincoln Shanghai

How to Beat the High Cost of Health Care
the "Total Benefits" Strategy

iUniverse books may be ordered through booksellers or by contacting:

iUniverse
2021 Pine Lake Road, Suite 100
Lincoln, NE 68512
www.iuniverse.com
1-800-Authors (1-800-288-4677)

ISBN: 0-595-34243-4

Printed in the United States of America

Contents

Introduction

Welcome to this discussion of "How to Beat the High Cost of Health Care." My name is Jennifer Nevin, and I'm with Total Benefits Consulting, LLC. We specialize in helping small to mid-size employers deliver affordable employee benefits. I'm here with my Total Benefits partners, Tom Quigley and Ed Lyon. Tom is also President of Total Benefits Planning, Inc. And Ed is also President of TaxTuneup.com, Inc. Today, we're going to discuss a two-prong strategy that Tom and Ed have developed to slash their clients' health-care costs up to 50%. Our goal is to help you decide whether their strategy can help cut your costs too.

Tom, let's start with you. Can you tell us a little bit about why health insurance rates keep going up?

Quigley: There are many reasons, but at this point the two biggest are rising prescription drug costs and improved technology investment.

Pharmaceutical companies enjoy patent protection for "blockbuster" drugs that drive up costs. They also advertise heavily, which influences doctors to prescribe brand-name drugs instead of generics. In 2003, Pfizer alone spent $13 on marketing for every man, woman, and child in the United States.

The second main driver is the cost of technology. Patients want the latest non-invasive tests and non-surgical "zappers." It's hard to control costs because we want the best health care possible. We just have to understand how quality drives costs. Other factors most people don't think of are the continuing aging of the population, effects of the baby boomer generation, fraud and abuse and increasing malpractice rates that affect doctor fees.

Nevin: How do you combat these rate increases?

Quigley: Ed and I show our clients a two-prong strategy that takes advantage of restructuring insurance coverage and a little-known tax break. I'll start by discussing insurance, then Ed will explain the tax aspects.

Most of my clients look for a single insurer to provide all of their coverage. It's certainly easier to write a single check—but this can be an expensive convenience. I ask my clients this:

"If you build a house, does the plumber build the whole house?"

The answer, of course, is "no." The client hires a general contractor, and the contractor outsources specific responsibilities to specific subcontractors.

Most employers aren't aware that they can create the same efficiencies with health insurance. Employers who adopt that mentality can really slash their costs. They do so by outsourcing coverage to supplemental carriers that specialize in specific risks such as outpatient and inpatient surgery—and do so more economically than major medical carriers.

Nevin: What is supplemental insurance?

Quigley: Supplemental insurance policies cover specific risks such as inpatient and outpatient surgery, accidents, and cancers. We counsel employers to raise the deductible on their primary coverage—then use supplemental insurance to fill in those gaps. This lets the employer offer "100%" health plans for less premium than major medical coverage.

This means buying coverage from two companies, not one. And it generally means more paperwork submitting claims. But the cost savings easily justify the extra administration. And our sister company, Total Benefits Administration, offers complete third-party administration services.

I would love to tell you we have a "magic bullet" that slashes insurance with no downside. But I doubt you'd believe me if I tried.

Nevin: Why does supplemental insurance save so much compared to primary carriers?

Quigley: Let me answer your question by drawing you a picture. Let's imagine that your health insurance coverage is provided in three main categories—three circles of coverage:

1. The first circle includes office visits, drug cards, doctors' appointments and trips to the emergency room. I call this "first dollar coverage." These are the day-to-day expenses most of us take for granted. And these are where your insurance company racks up most of their administrative costs.

2. The second circle includes inpatient and outpatient testing, such as CAT scans and MRIs, and inpatient and outpatient surgeries. These are the big expenses we count on insurance to cover. These would be real wallet-busters if you had to cover them yourselves—but insurers can price them realistically.

3. The third circle includes catastrophic care—birth defects, long-term chemotherapy, organ transplants, and genuine medical disasters. Major medical carriers can be on the hook for $1 million, $2 million, and even $5 million maximum benefits here—and they're forced to set aside reserves for these uncertain risks.

Most employers choose one carrier to cover all these risks. But you can save big by outsourcing the second circle to supplemental insurers. They avoid the day-to-day costs of administering "first circle" coverage. And they avoid the tremendous financial risks of "third circle" coverage. This lets their actuaries price their coverage far more efficiently.

Nevin: Do supplemental insurers cover experimental treatments?

Quigley: Most policies cover experimental treatments, while others exclude them. It's always important to read the policy and understand what you are buying. This type of coverage is a nice alternative to taking a second mortgage out on a house to pay for a benefit not usually covered by "first dollar" policies.

Nevin: Do employers need to switch carriers to take advantage of this strategy?

Quigley: In most cases, you don't have to switch carriers. Most carriers offer higher-deductible plans you can choose. The growth in Health Savings Accounts means more carriers will offer more choices. You may have to wait until you renew to switch—but you're not likely to have to leave.

If your employees are healthy, you may want to explore options with other carriers. Switching may save you even more. But it's generally not necessary.

Nevin: Let's turn our attention now to Ed Lyon and the tax aspects of the strategy. Ed, How does the tax code help employers and self-employed individuals?

Lyon: Now we are working on the second prong of the 2-part strategy. The tax code really doesn't give employers and self-employed individuals as much help as you would think.

1. Employer-provided health insurance is tax-free for employees. That is the biggest single benefit in the tax code.

2. If you're self-employed, not covered by another employer's subsidized plan, you can write off 100% of your health insurance (including long-term care, Medicare Part "B", and so-called "Medigap" policies) as an adjustment to gross income.

3. Finally, you can write off medical and dental expenses as an itemized deduction—so long as you itemize, and only to the extent they exceed 7.5% of your "adjusted gross income," or AGI. (That means, for example, if your adjusted gross income is $100,000, you can only itemize deductions medical and dental expenses that exceed $7,500.) But most taxpayers don't itemize. That means they don't get a chance to deduct

their health care costs. And most taxpayers who do itemize don't spend more than 7.5% of AGI on health care.

Nevin: The tax code certainly doesn't seem to offer much help. I've heard a lot about the new Health Savings Accounts, or HSAs. What exactly are these accounts, and how do they work?

Lyon: HSAs are a strategy for using the tax code to help solve health care costs. The concept here is pretty straightforward. Employers provide health insurance with high deductibles and out-of-pocket maximums. Currently, those deductibles are at least $1,000 for individual policies and $2,000 for family coverage. These policies are less expensive than "first-dollar coverage" for the reasons Tom explained just a few minutes ago when he covered the first prong of the strategy. Employees then make tax-deductible contributions to the actual HSA and use money from that account to pay for their health care expenses. They can contribute 100% of the policy deductible, up to $2,600 for individuals and $5,200 for families each year.

This lets employees deduct their out-of-pocket expenses, without the usual 7.5% limit, because they deduct the original contributions from the HSA. But HSAs pose three real problems:

First, eligibility is limited. Both you and, if you're married, your spouse have to be covered by a "high deductible health policy," or HDHP.

Second, you have to pre-fund the account before you can take money out of it. Employees have a hard enough time saving for retirement, the kids' college, and the house on the lake without having to save for trips to the dentist.

And third, some health-care costs, like braces for your kids' teeth and fertility treatments, may cost more than your maximum contribution to the account. For those expenses, you're back where you started—out of luck.

So the HSAs are a first effort at using the tax code to help bring down the high cost of health care, but they aren't a very satisfactory solution. And frankly, employees are going to be disappointed when they realize these limits.

Nevin: What happens if you don't use all the money that you put in an HSA account?

Lyon: The health savings account lets you save that money and carry it over. In fact, some financial planners recommend using HSAs as supplemental retirement plan accounts. You can even open a "self-directed" HSA that lets you buy real estate in your account! But money that goes into the HSA stays in the HSA—it doesn't come out except for health care costs. If you take money out of the HSA and use it for anything other than medical expenses, you are going to pay the tax on it that you saved going in.

Nevin: What about cafeteria plans? Don't they give employees a tax break for health-care costs?

Lyon: Section 125 plans—also called "cafeteria plans"—are a more familiar tax benefit plan for larger employers. Cafeteria plans let employees contribute pre-tax dollars to segregated accounts for health care costs. You deduct money from your paycheck every month, it goes into the account and you use those pre-tax dollars "tax-free" to pay for your medical expenses.

But cafeteria plans have disadvantages as well. First, just as with HSAs, you have to pre-fund your account. Your employer may be deducting money today for expenses that you are not going to need until down the road. Second, you have to use all the money in your cafeteria plan by the end of the year or you lose it. And that's a scary thought. You might have a $1,000 to $2,000 sitting in your cafeteria plan in November or December. If you don't use that money by the end of the year—you lose it! That's why a lot of people buy prescription sunglasses in December. Third, you have to decide ahead of time how much to contribute to your account. Once you make that decision, you're generally stuck with it. So big expenses like a Lasik eye surgery or braces for your kids' teeth may not be covered.

Nevin: Let's talk about the Section 105 medical expense reimbursement plan. What exactly is a Section 105 plan, and how does it work?

Lyon: The Section 105 plan has been around since 1954, but has become increasingly popular as a solution to the disadvantages of a medical savings account and the cafeteria plan.

A Section 105 plan is simply a written plan that lets employers deduct amounts they pay to reimburse employees, tax-free, for medical and dental costs they incur on behalf of themselves, their spouses, and their dependents. That's a mouthful, so let's take it step-by-step.

1. First, you'll need a written plan. That's easy enough. We provide our clients with a complete package, including plan documents, summary plan descriptions, ERISA, HIPAA, FMLA, and COBRA disclosures, and administrative forms.

2. Second, the plan has to cover employees. Now, if you're self-employed, as a sole proprietor or member of a single-person LLC (taxed as a proprietorship), you might think you're out of luck. Not to worry! If you're married, hire your spouse to perform bona fide service under a written

employment contract. If you're not married, incorporate as a "C" corporation, and hire yourself. If you operate as an "S" corporation, you can't cover yourself or your spouse. But you can still cover your employees. And you might be able to "peel off" a specific source of income as a proprietorship or "C" corporation, and pay benefits through that entity.

3.   Third, the plan reimburses employees for expenses they incur for themselves, their spouses, and their dependents. Remember when I suggested you hire your spouse? That lets you cover your spouse—their spouse, meaning you—and their dependents. That's how you establish the plan to cover yourself.

One national organization that sponsors Section 105 plans for its members estimates they save an average of $1,800 to $2,500 per year, depending on their tax bracket. But I've seen self-employed clients save as much as $10,000 in a single year.

Nevin: How does a Section 105 plan benefit larger employers?

Lyon: Self-employed individuals use Section 105 as a tax shelter. Larger employers use it as a true employee benefit. That's because the plan lets them self-insure risks they would otherwise have to pay an insurance company to assume.

If you adopt a 105 plan, you can use all sorts of strategies to deliver benefits:

- You can use the plan as an accounting device to reimburse employees or their health-care providers on an as-needed basis. Employees will submit reimbursements, monthly, quarterly, or as frequently as you choose. There's no need to establish a separate account or pre-fund expenses as there is with an HSA or cafeteria plan. And our third-party administrator handles employee claims.

- You can establish employee accounts and contribute periodically as you choose. These are called "healthcare reimbursement accounts," or HRAs. And the IRS just gave them a big boost by clarifying that, unlike with cafeteria plans, account balances can roll over from year to year.

- You can even give employees debit cards that they can use for qualified expenses!

- You'll determine what expenses are eligible for reimbursement when you set up the plan. You can choose to reimburse all health care expenses up to a certain dollar amount or choose to reimburse just some health care expenses.

- Your maximum reimbursement per employee determines your maximum out-of-pocket risk. If you're moving from a traditional "first-dollar" health insurance plan, you can raise the deductible on your insurance and cover the gap yourself. Or you can raise the deductible, supplement that plan with Gap insurance policies, and then use the Section 105 to fill-in places that might be left between the Gap insurance and the primary health care plan. You have total flexibility to design the plan and nearly total flexibility to fund it and reimburse your employees.

Nevin: That does sound like a better way!

Lyon: Our two-prong strategy isn't for everyone. But when it fits, it saves big. Our clients generally save 20–50% on overall health-care costs. And that's a savings no employer can afford to miss!

The "Total Benefits" Strategy Illustrated

If you think it costs too much to stay healthy, I've got bad news and I've got good news. The bad news, of course, is that you're right—it does cost too much! The good news is, it doesn't have to—*if* you have a better strategy.

Health care costs swallow nearly 1 out of every 6 dollars in today's economy. In 2002, that meant $4,550 for every man, woman, and child. Figures for 2003 aren't yet available. But they didn't go down.

In the next few minutes, we'll illustrate how using the "Total Benefits" strategy can cut costs by 20–50% per year, without cutting benefits. In most cases, without changing insurance companies. It works for businesses from 1 employee to 1,000. It works for all types of businesses too, including schools, government entities, nonprofits and churches. Take a look, and see how it can work for you!

Health Care Spending Quiz

Match the spending items to the right costs. No peeking!

A. 2003 Team Payroll:
   Super Bowl Champ New England Patriots   1. $74,700,000

B. 2003 Salary + Bonus:
   UnitedHealthcare CEO Bill McGuire   2. $94,200,000

C. 2003 spending (per citizen):
   U.S. Military, Ammunition Budget   3. $12

D. 2003 spending (per citizen):
   Pfizer, Inc. Drug Marketing Budget   4. $13

(c)2004, Total Benefits Consulting LLC. All rights reserved.

Health Care Cost Quiz:

We'll start with a quick health care cost quiz. Can you match each of these spending items to the right cost?

It's easy. "A" matches "1," "B" matches "2," "C" matches "3," and "D" matches "4."

That's right, the chairman of one insurance company made more than the New England Patriots. But he didn't win a Super Bowl.

And yes, Pfizer spent more on drug marketing than the entire United States Armed Forces spent on ammunition. And Pfizer didn't win a war.

Family Premium Costs:

Now that I've got your attention, let's see how employers can protect themselves from these ridiculous costs.

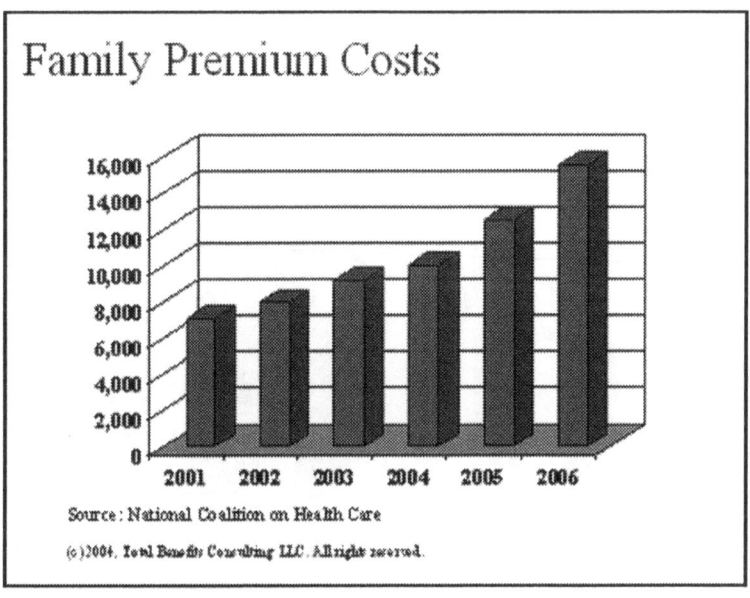

Family Premium Costs

16,000	
14,000	
12,000	
10,000	
8,000	
6,000	
4,000	
2,000	
0	2001 2002 2003 2004 2005 2006

Source: National Coalition on Health Care

(c)2004, Total Benefits Consulting LLC. All rights reserved.

Where Your Premium Dollars Go:

Soaring health care premiums don't even make front page news. The National Coalition on Health Care reports that the average family premium, which stood at $9,160 in 2003, will climb to $15,545 by 2006. How can you afford to stay in the game? What will you do when your insurance costs more than your house?

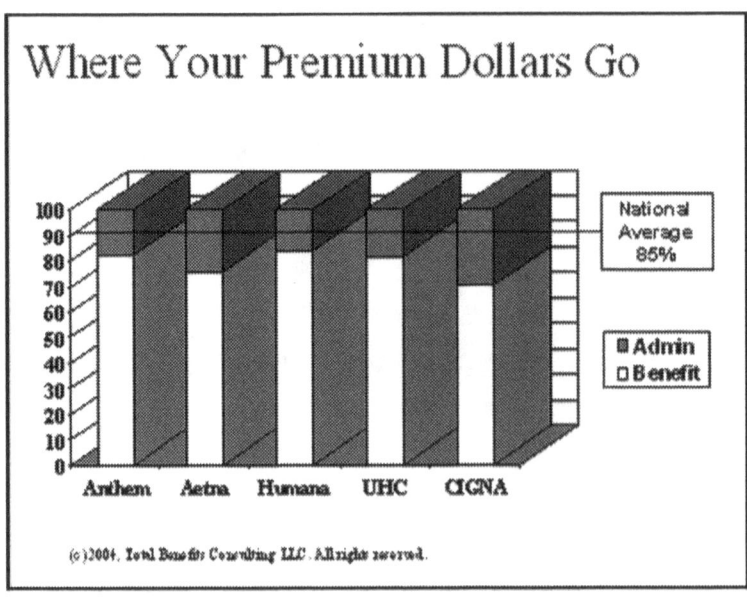

If you're responsible for health care benefits, for yourself, your family, or your employees, you're assuming a tremendous risk. Accidents, cancers, premature births, and the like, can cost hundreds of thousands of dollars. If you're like most employers, you can't afford to bear that risk yourself. So you finance it, through monthly insurance premiums.

Buying health insurance is like buying your house. You probably didn't write a check for the full price. You financed it, and you make monthly payments. But you're not locked into those payments. You can refinance your loan to take advantage of lower rates. You can add a home equity loan or line of credit to improve your house. If you bought your house before interest rates dropped to record lows, you're probably paying less every month, for the same house.

The problem with buying health insurance is that it costs more than buying benefits. Your insurance company collects what they need to pay those benefits, plus their costs for administration and profit. Nationwide, a dollar of group health insurance premium delivers about 85 cents worth of benefits. Is there some way we can cut out this "middleman," and deliver better benefits? Fortunately, there is. The Total Benefits strategy lets you "refinance" your health care plan, without cutting benefits.

If you own your own home, you buy homeowners' insurance. But you don't buy it for a $50 plumber's bill. Otherwise, it would cost a fortune! If you own a car, you have car insurance. But you don't buy it for a $40 oil change. Again, it would cost a fortune! Raising your health care deductible works the same way, and it saves a fortune. That's the first step of the strategy. But that leaves the challenge of replacing benefits. Now lets look at how we replace them.

Step One: Raising Deductibles:

The first step is simply raising deductibles. This is the same strategy that so many employers are turning to in order to offer the new Health Savings Accounts. We've seen employers slash premiums by up to 48% or more.

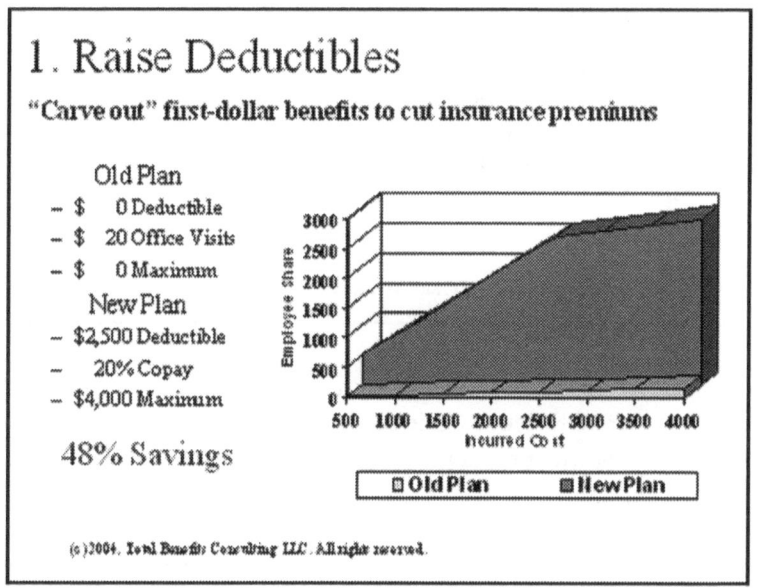

Step Two: Adding Section 105 Plan:

The next step is adding a Section 105 plan.

The Section 105 plan lets you decide, within limits, who is eligible, and what to reimburse. You can't discriminate in favor of highly compensated employees. But you can use a classification test, such as "all participants in your group health plan." And you can exclude part-time, seasonal, short-term, and younger employees. If you operate your business as a sole proprietorship, you can even hire your spouse and pay benefits through them!

2. Buy Back Benefits

Add §105(b) plan to reimburse employees for lost benefits

Define Eligible Employees	Define/Deliver Benefits
• Must be nondiscriminatory • May use "classification" test: – "all participants in Employer's group health plan" • "Safe harbor" exclusions: – Less than 25 hours/week – Less than 7 months/year – Less than 3 years service – Age 25 or under	• Define eligible expenses – Copays, deductibles, R – Diagnostic/testing – Dental/vision/chiropractic – "Any eligible expense under IRC Section 213(d)" • Deliver benefits – Pay health care providers – Reimburse employees directly

(c)2004, Total Benefits Consulting LLC. All rights reserved.

You decide what to cover, and how much to pay. You can cover any qualifying expense under Internal Revenue Code Section 213. Any kind of health insurance. Major medical, supplemental, and long-term care insurance. Copays, deductibles, and prescriptions. Dental, vision, and chiropractic care. Big-ticket items like braces for your children's teeth, fertility treatments, and special schools for learning-disabled children. You can even cover nonprescription medications and supplies.

You can reimburse your employees, or pay health care providers directly. You can administer it yourself, or hire a third-party administrator (TPA). At Total Benefits, we offer an in-house third-party administrator with specialized TPA software designed specifically for high-deductible health plans.

Third Step: Insure Your Savings:

The third step, which we recommend for new plans, is to add supplemental insurance for specific risks like accidents and surgeries. These plans won't cover everything you trade off when you raise your deductible. But that's not what they're intended to do. The purpose here is to insure your savings and smooth out your cash flow so that bigger expenses don't hit at once. Smaller employers generally keep supplemental insurance for this reason, while larger employers may choose to forego this coverage.

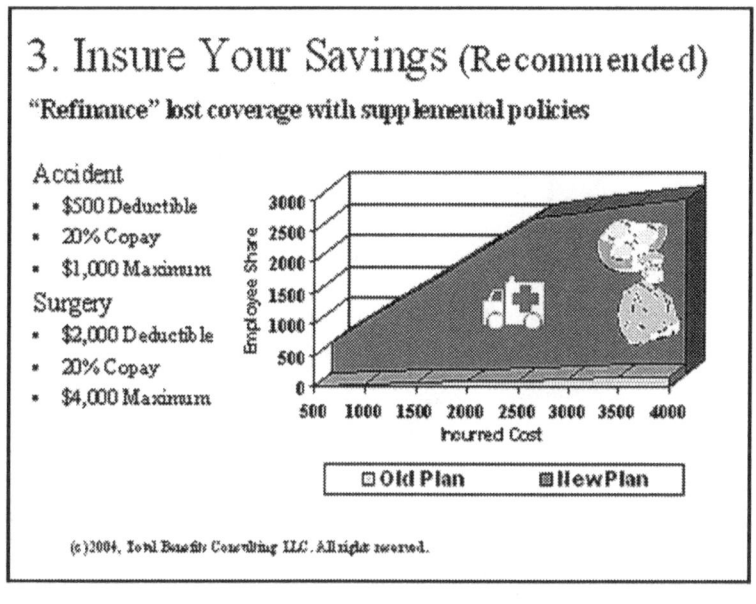

Total Benefits Summary:

We tell our clients that designing a health plan is like raising a roof. The major medical plan is like the frame that holds the roof together. Supplemental and individual plans are like the insulation and panels that keep out the weather. And the 105 plan is like the shingles that prevent leaks. You count on your builder to give you all three. Count on Total Benefits to do the same for your employees—Typically for 20–50% less. What can you do with your savings?

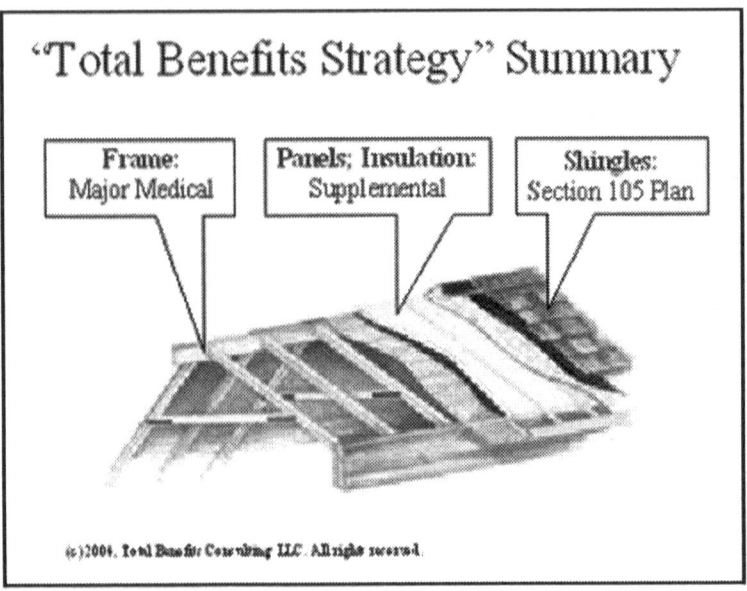

Optional Steps: Individual Piece and Spousal 105

We offer two more optional pieces for appropriate clients. With the "individual piece," we actually take healthy spouses and dependents off the group plan, and write individual policies. This offers several advantages:

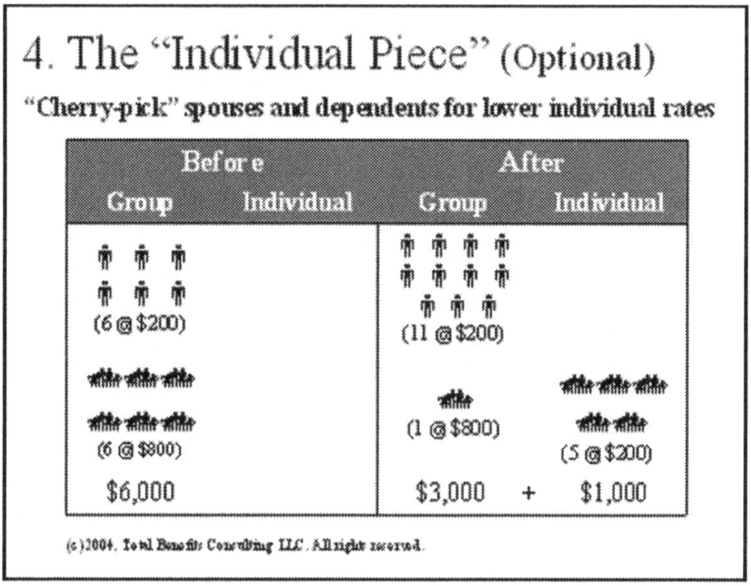

4. The "Individual Piece" (Optional)

"Cherry-pick" spouses and dependents for lower individual rates

Before		After	
Group	Individual	Group	Individual
�♦ ♦ ♦ ♦ ♦ ♦ (6 @ $200)		♦ ♦ ♦ ♦ ♦ ♦ ♦ ♦ ♦ ♦ ♦ (11 @ $200)	
🧑🧑🧑 🧑🧑🧑 (6 @ $800)		🧑 (1 @ $800)	🧑🧑🧑 🧑🧑 (5 @ $200)
$6,000		$3,000	+ $1,000

(c)2004. Total Benefits Consulting LLC. All rights reserved.

- Healthy spouses and dependents get lower rates than for the group as a whole.
- Their health experience no longer affects group rates.
- Families who leave the company can take their coverage with them, regardless of COBRA continuation rules.

We're very careful, when we add the individual piece, to make sure that all employees and their dependents have group coverage in place before adding individual policies. Spouses and dependents have to qualify for individual coverage *before* we move them out of the group plan. And we won't do it without making sure that third-party administrative services are in place.

5. "Spousal 105" (Optional)

Redefine eligibility to avoid double-coverage; reimburse with §105

Before	After
👤 👤 👤 👤 👤 👤 👤 👤 👤 (9 @ $200)	👤 👤 👤 👤 👤 👤 👤 👤 (8 @ $200)
👪 👪 👪 👪 👪 👪 👪 👪 👪 (9 @ $800)	👪 👪 👪 (3 @ $800)
$9,000	$4,000 + §105

The final piece is the "spousal 105," which avoids duplicate coverage for married couples. First, we redefine eligibility for the group plan to require employees who are eligible for coverage under a spouse's plan to elect that coverage. Then we reimburse them directly for any expenses not covered by their spouse's plan. This way, the couple gets better benefits than they could under either plan individually, *without* the cost of duplicating coverage.

What About Health Savings Accounts?

Health Savings Accounts, or HSAs, are attracting a lot of attention. But we find that most employers looking to cut costs without cutting benefits prefer our strategy. Here's why:

- HSAs force you to buy specified high-deductible insurance. And spousal coverage can make employees ineligible for the savings account.

- HSAs have to be prefunded. There are specific monthly and annual funding limits that can make it hard to get money into the accounts to use for eligible expenses.

- Employers who fund their employees' accounts can watch employees leave the company and take the account with them. With health care coverage, so tight, the last thing most employers want is to fund health savings accounts that don't get used for health!

- Finally, HDHP don't permit prescription drug benefits until after the deductible is met. This means employees lose the drug-card benefits they've grown to count on.

§105 vs. HSA

Feature	§105	HSA
Benefit?	Limited only by Employer	Limited to major-medical deductible
Eligibility?	Defined by Employer	May be limited
Pre-funding?	Not required	Required
Portable?	None	Fully Vested And Portable

(c)2004. Total Benefits Consulting LLC. All right reserved.

How Does the Reimbursement Process Work?

The Section 105 medical expense reimbursement plan lets you reimburse employees on an as-needed basis for expenses they incur for themselves, their spouses, and their dependents. This lets you pay just a dollar for a dollar's worth of benefits, when your employees need it.

Reimbursement Process

Before	After
Provider submits bill to Insurer	Same
Insurer determines coverage	Same
Insurer reimburses Provider	Same
Insurer submits EOB to Employee	Same
	Employee submits EOB to TBA
	TBA determines 105 coverage
	TBA/Employer reimburse Provider
	TBA submits bill to "Gap" Insurer
	"Gap" carrier determines coverage
	"Gap" carrier reimburses Employer
Employee pays balance	Same

(c)2004, Total Benefits Consulting LLC. All rights reserved.

We've streamlined administration to make employee reimbursements as easy as possible. Employees have just one additional step, which is to submit the "Explanation of Benefits" for covered services to Total Benefits Administration. TBA determines coverage, reimburses providers, and submits claims to supplemental insurers.

```
┌─────────────────────────────────────────────────────────────────┐
│                                                                   │
│  Client Example        ┌────────────────────────────────┐        │
│                        │ Manufacturer                   │        │
│                        │ 10 Employees – single          │        │
│                        │ 20 Employees – with family     │        │
│                        └────────────────────────────────┘        │
│                                                                   │
│   Before – per month            After – per month                │
│  ────────────────────          ─────────────────────             │
│   $20,000 major medical         $12,000 major medical             │
│                                 $ 2,500 gap                       │
│                                 $ 1,000 §105 allowance            │
│   $20,000 total                 $15,500 total                     │
│                                                                   │
│                                       ⬭ $4,500/month ⬮            │
│                                         Savings                   │
│                                                                   │
│  (c)2004. Total Benefits Consulting LLC. All right reserved.      │
└─────────────────────────────────────────────────────────────────┘
```

Let's take a look at an actual client to see just how the process works. Our client is a Cincinnati specialty products manufacturer with 30 employees. They were paying $20,000/month to insure their employees and families. We raised their out-of-pocket maximum to $5,000, which cut their major medical premium by 40%. We added back in gap insurance to cover accident and surgery risk, at $2,500/month. Then we installed a Section 105 plan to "mop up" any unreimbursed costs. This plan costs about $1,000/month. Together, these strategies saved $4,500/month, or $54,000/year. This employer could save even more by buying individual coverage and installing a spousal 105.

Final Steps:

Now it's your turn. Do you want to save 20–50% on health care costs, without cutting benefits? At Total Benefits, we meet with clients and their accountants to see just what we can save. If we move forward, we start with an "agent of record" letter and 105 plan installation agreement. If not, we'll part friends.

Don't let soaring health care costs threaten your organization's financial security. With the "Total Benefits" strategy, the choice truly is yours. Make a decision today!

Sources

Rev. Rul. 71-588

Code Secs. 105, 162

26 CFR 1.105-2: Amounts expended for medical care.
(Also Section 162; 1.162-10.)

Amounts reimbursed under an accident and health plan covering all bona fide employees, including the owner's wife, and their families are not includible in the employee's gross income and are deductible by the owner as business expenses.

The taxpayer operated a business as a sole proprietorship with several bona fide full-time employees including his wife. The taxpayer had an accident and health plan covering all employees and their families. During 1970 two employees, including the wife, incurred expenses for medical care for themselves, their spouses, and their children, and were reimbursed pursuant to the plan. The reimbursed amounts qualified both as amounts received under an accident or health plan for employees within the meaning of section 105(e) of the Internal Revenue Code of 1954 and as amounts described in section 105(b) of the Code.

Held, the reimbursed amounts received by the employees are not includible in their gross income pursuant to section 105(b) of the Code and these amounts are deductible by the taxpayer as a business expense under section 162(a) of the Code.

<<END RULING>>

Private Letter Ruling 9409006

ISSUES:

1. Whether A, a sole proprietor, is entitled to deduct under section 162(a) of the Internal Revenue Code, amounts paid to B, A's spouse and employee, as reimbursement of medical expenses under an employer-provided accident or health plan.

2. Whether amounts B receives as reimbursement of expenses that B incurs on behalf of B, A, and their dependents are excluded from B's gross income under section 105(b).

FACTS:

A operates a consulting business as a sole proprietor and employs B, A's spouse, to perform certain services in connection with the business. B receives compensation for the services B performs and includes the compensation in gross income on the couple's jointly-filed federal income tax return. A adopted a written employer-provided accident and health plan that, by its terms, covers all employees of A's business. During the year in question, A reimbursed B, pursuant to the plan, for the expenses of medical care that incurred on behalf of B, A, and their dependents. You agreed that there is a bona fide employer-employee relationship between A and B.

LAW:

Section 162(a) of the Code allows a deduction for all the ordinary and necessary expenses paid or incurred during the taxable year in carrying on a trade or business, including reasonable salaries and other compensation for services rendered.

Section 213(a) of the Code allows a deduction for the expenses paid during the taxable year, not compensated by insurance or otherwise, for medical care of the taxpayer, the taxpayer's spouse, or a dependent, to the extent that such expenses exceed 7.5% of the taxpayer's AGI. The term "medical care" is defined in section 213(d).

Section 105(b) of the Code generally allows an employee to exclude from gross income employer-paid reimbursements for the expenses of medical care (as defined in section 213(d)) of the employee and the employee's spouse and dependents.

Rev. Rul. 71-588, 1971-2 C.B. 91, holds that amounts paid by a sole proprietor to his spouse, a bona fide employee of the business, under an accident and health plan covering all employees are (1) excludable from the employee-spouse's gross income under section 105(b) of the Code and (2) deductible by the employer-spouse as a business expense under section 162(a).

CONCLUSION:

Applying the law to the facts of the present case, the amounts paid to B under the plan as reimbursement for medical expenses are deductible by A as a business expense under section 162(a) of the Code. Further, B may exclude these amounts from gross income under section 105(b).

UIL 162.35-02

Effective Date: March 29, 1999

ISSUES:

1. Where an employer, who is self-employed, provides accident and health coverage to his spouse as an employee, is the cost of that coverage deductible by the employer-spouse under section 162 of the Internal Revenue Code.

2. Where an employer, who is self-employed, provides accident and health coverage to his spouse as an employee, is the cost of that coverage and medical reimbursements excludable by the employee under sections 106 and 105(b) of the Code.

CONCLUSIONS:

1. The cost of the accident and health coverage is deductible by the employer spouse if he provides such coverage to his spouse as an employee.

2. Both the cost of the coverage and the medical reimbursements are excludable from the gross income of the employee-spouse.

STATEMENT OF FACTS:

An arrangement is marketed through accounting firms and a national tax return preparer that encourages self-employed persons to deduct 100% of accident and health plan expenses. This arrangement has been utilized by the self-employed in partnerships, limited liability corporations, subchapter S corporations and sole proprietorships. Through this promotion, a self-employed individual hires his or her spouse as an employee. The employer-spouse provides family accident and health coverage for the employee-spouse through a self-insured medical expense reimbursement plan or by purchasing an accident and health insurance policy. The employer-spouse is then covered by the plan as a member of the employee's family.

By utilizing this arrangement, the employer-spouse deducts 100% of the cost of providing health coverage to himself and his family, including reimbursement of medical expenses. Expenses claimed for reimbursement include insurance premiums and other expenses not reimbursed by insurance. The employee-spouse excludes from gross income the cost of the health coverage and medical expense reimbursements.

Often, compensation for the employee-spouse is determined upon the amount of the accident and health cost for the taxable year. In this situation, Form W-2 is not issued or is issued for a small dollar amount because the cost of the coverage and medical expense reimbursements are excluded from the employee-spouse's income.

LAW AND ANALYSIS:

ISSUE 1:

Section 162(a)(1) of the Code provides that a taxpayer may deduct all the ordinary and necessary expenses paid or incurred during the taxable year in carrying on any trade or business, including a reasonable allowance for salaries or other compensation for personal services actually rendered.

Section 1.162-7(a) of the Income Tax Regulations provides that there shall be included among the ordinary and necessary expenses paid or incurred in carrying on any trade or business a reasonable allowance for salaries or other compensation for services actually rendered. The test of deductibility in the case of compensation payments is whether they are reasonable and are in fact payments purely for services.

Section 1.162-10(a) of the regulations provides, in part, that amounts paid or incurred within the taxable year for dismissal wages, unemployment benefits, guaranteed annual wages, vacations, or a sickness, accident, hospitalization, medical expense, recreational, welfare or similar benefit plan (other than deferred compensation plans referred to in section 404 of the Code) are deductible under section 162(a) if they are ordinary and necessary expenses of the trade or business.

Section 262(a) provides that except as otherwise provided, no deduction shall be allowed for personal, living, or family expenses.

In Rev. Rul. 71-588, 1971-2 C.B. 91, the taxpayer operated a business as a sole proprietorship with several bona fide full-time employees, including his wife. The taxpayer had a self-insured accident and health plan that covered all employees and their families. During 1970, two of the employees, including the wife, incurred expenses for medical care for themselves, their spouses and their children, and were reimbursed pursuant to the plan. Under these facts, the Service held that the amounts paid in reimbursement were deductible by the taxpayer as business expenses under section 162 of the Code and excludable by the employees (including the wife) under section 105(b) of the Code.

Accordingly, the Service's position is that the cost of accident and health coverage, including medical expense reimbursements, are deductible by the employer-spouse if the employee-spouse is determined to be a bona fide employee of the business under the common law rules or otherwise provides services to the business for which the accident and health coverage is reasonable compensation. However, if the "employee-spouse" does not meet this standard, the accident and health coverage is a personal expense under section 262(a) of the Code, which is not deductible under section 162(a). Other Code provisions apply in this situation.

Section 213(a) allows a deduction for expenses paid during the taxable year, not compensated for by insurance or otherwise, for medical care of the taxpayer, his spouse, or a dependent to the extent that such expenses exceed 7.5 percent of adjusted gross income.

Section 162(l) provides, in the case of a self-employed individual, there shall be allowed an amount equal to the applicable percentage under this section of the amount paid during the taxable year for insurance which constitutes medical care for the taxpayer, his spouse, and dependents. If the "employee-spouse" is not an employee of the "employer-spouse's" business, or does not otherwise provide services to the business, the cost of accident and health insurance purchased by the "employer-spouse" is deductible by the employer-spouse only up to the applicable percentage under section 162(l) of the Code. The cost of insurance in excess of the applicable percentage is deductible to the extent permitted under section 213(a) of the Code. In addition, if the "employee-spouse" is not an employee of the "employer-spouse's" business or does not otherwise provide services to the business, amounts paid by the "employer-spouse" for the reimbursement of medical expenses under the self-insured plan for himself, his spouse, and his dependents are only deductible to the extent provided under section 213(a) of the Code.

Note that if an accident and health insurance policy is purchased in the name of the employer-spouse the limitations of section 162(l) of the Code apply, notwithstanding that the policy provides coverage for the employer-spouse, the employee-spouse and their dependents.

ISSUE 2:

Section 104(a)(3) of the Code provides that, except in the case of amounts attributable to and not in excess of deductions allowed under section 213, gross income does not include amounts received through accident or health insurance (or through an arrangement having the effect of accident or health insurance) for personal injuries or sickness other than amounts received by an employee, to the extent such amounts (A) are attributable to contributions by the employer which were not includible in the gross income of the employee, or (B) are paid by the employer.

Section 106(a) of the Code provides that gross income of an employee does not include employer-provided coverage under an accident and health plan.

Section 105(a) of the Code provides that, generally, amounts received by an employee through accident and health insurance for personal injuries or sickness shall be included in gross income to the extent such amounts (1) are attributable to contributions by the employer which were not includible in the gross income of the employee, or (2) are paid by the employer.

Section 105(b) of the Code provides an exception to the general rule of inclusion under section 105(a). Section 105(b) states that gross income does not include amounts referred to in subsection (a) (employer-provided accident and health insurance) if such amounts are paid, directly or indirectly, to the employee to reimburse the employee for expenses incurred by him, his spouse or dependents for medical care.

Section 105(e) provides that amounts received under an accident or health plan for employees shall be treated as amounts received through accident or health insurance for purpose of sections 105(a) and (b).

Accordingly, because self-insured medical expense reimbursement plans are treated as accident and health insurance under section 105(e), medical expense reimbursements paid under such plans are excludable from the employee's gross income under section 105(b) (to the extent benefits do not discriminate in favor of highly compensated individuals under section 105(h)).

The Service's position is that the cost of accident and health coverage or medical expense reimbursement is excludable from gross income by the employee-spouse only if the employee-spouse is a bona fide employee under the common law rules. If the "employee spouse" is not a bona fide employee, then the cost of accident and health coverage provided by the "employer-spouse" is not excluded from the gross income of the "employee-spouse" under section 106(a) of the Code, because the section 106 exclusion only applies to the "gross income of an employee." Similarly, medical expense reimbursements received by the "employee-spouse" are not excluded from gross income under section 105(b) of the Code. However, if the cost of accident and health coverage provided by the "employer-spouse" is included in the "employee-spouse's" gross income, all amounts received by the "employee-spouse" and family for personal injury and sickness under the coverage are excludable under section 104(a)(3).

An additional factor to consider in this situation is the eligibility provisions of a self insured accident or health plan. The adoption agreement and plan document must provide that the employee-spouse is eligible to participate. For example, very often a specific service requirement applies to current employees as well as new employees. This waiting period may not have been applied to the employee-spouse, but may have been used to exclude other employees. Thus, if it is not documented that the employee-spouse has met the service requirement, the employee-spouse may not participate and medical expense reimbursements would not be excludable under section 105(b) because they would not be received under an accident and health plan.

In addition, if the service requirement has not been consistently applied to all employees, the self-insured plan could be discriminatory under section 105(h).

Whether the "employee-spouse" is an employee, must be determined on a case-by case basis. See Attachment for additional guidance.

The extent and nature of the spouse's involvement in the business operations are critical. Although, part-time work does not negate employee status, the performance of nominal or insignificant services that have no economic substance or independent significance may be challenged. Merely calling a spouse an "employee" is not sufficient to qualify a non-working spouse as an employee.

In addition, a spouse may be a self-employed individual engaged in the trade or business as a joint owner, co-owner, or partner. For example, a significant investment of the spouse's separate funds in (or significant co-ownership or joint ownership of) the business assets may support a finding that the spouse is self-employed in the business rather than an employee.

Marital property or community property laws that give a spouse an ownership interest in a business operated by a self-employed individual may be relevant, but not necessarily conclusive, for determining whether the spouse is also self-employed in that business. Note that state laws that impose on one family member a legal obligation to support another family member are generally irrelevant in determining the tax treatment of fringe benefits. See, Rev. Rul. 73-393, 1973-2 C.B. 33.

Under sections 318 and 1372 of the Code, a spouse of more than a 2-percent shareholder of a subchapter S corporation is treated as more than a 2-percent shareholder for certain employee fringe benefit purposes, including accident and health benefits. Thus, both the spouse and the more than 2-percent shareholder are treated as partners in a partnership for benefit purposes. See, Rev. Rul. 91-26,

1991-1 C.B. 184. For the tax treatment of limited liability corporations, see Rev. Rul. 88-76, 1988-2 C.B. 360.

INDUSTRY'S ARGUMENTS:

Promoters of this arrangement do not dispute the assertion that the critical issue is whether the "employee-spouse" is a bona fide employee of the "employer-spouse's" business. If the employee-spouse is a bona fide employee, then Rev. Rul. 71-588 is applicable for purposes of deductibility and income tax exclusion.

ATTACHMENT

The following is a brief outline of the law regarding employment status. It is important to note that either worker classification—independent contractor or employee—can be valid. For an in-depth discussion, see the training material "Independent Contractor or Employee?" Training 3320-102 (Rev. 10-96) TPDS 842381, for determining employment status. The training materials are also available on the IRS home page on the Internet at http://www.irs.ustreas.gov.

In determining a worker's status, the primary inquiry is whether the worker is an independent contractor or an employee under the common law standard. Under the common law, the treatment of a worker as an independent contractor or an employee originates from the legal definitions developed in the law of agency—whether one party, the principal, is legally responsible for the acts or omissions of another party, the agent—and depends on the principa's right to direct and control the agent.

Guidelines for determining a worker's employment status are found in three substantially similar sections of the Employment Tax Regulations: sections 31.3121(d)-1, 31.3306(i)-1, and 34.3401(c)-1, relating to the Federal Insurance Contributions Act (FICA), the Federal Unemployment Tax Act (FUTA), and federal income tax withholding. The regulations provide that an employer-employee relationship exists when the business for which the services are performed has the right to direct and control the worker who performs the services. This control refers not only to the result to be accomplished by the work, but also to the means and details by which that result is accomplished. In other words, a worker is subject to the will and control of the business not only as to what work shall be done but also how it shall be done. It is not necessary that the employer actually direct or control the manner in which the services are performed; it is sufficient if the employer has the right to do so. To determine whether the control test is satisfied in a particular case, the facts and circumstances must be examined.

The Service now looks at facts in the following categories when determining worker classification: behavioral control, financial control and relationship of the parties.

Behavioral Control

Facts that substantiate the right to direct or control the details and means by which the worker performs the required services are considered under behavioral control. This includes factors such as training and instructions provided by the business. Virtually every business will impose on workers, whether independent contractors or employees, some form of instruction (for example, requiring that the job be performed within specified time frames). This fact alone is not sufficient evidence to determine the worker's status. The weight of "instructions" in any case depends on the degree to which instructions apply to how the job gets done rather than to the end result. The degree of instruction depends on the scope of instructions, the extent to which the business retains the right to control the worker's compliance with the instructions, and the effect on the worker in the event of noncompliance. The more detailed the instructions that the worker is required to follow, the more control the business exercises over the worker, and the more likely the business retains the right to control the methods by which the worker performs the work. The absence of detail in instructions reflects less control.

Financial Control

Whether the business has the right to direct or control the economic aspects of the worker's activities should be analyzed to determine worker status. Economic aspects of a relationship between the parties illustrate who has financial control of the activities undertaken. The items that usually need to be explored are whether the worker has a significant investment, unreimbursed expenses, whether the worker's services are available to the relevant market, the method of payment and opportunity for profit or loss. The first four items are not only important in their own right but also affect whether there is an opportunity for the realization of profit or loss. All of these can be thought of as bearing on the issue of whether the recipient has the right to direct and control the means and details of the business aspects of how the worker performs services.

The ability to realize a profit or incur a loss is probably the strongest evidence that a worker controls the business aspects of services rendered. Significant investment, unreimbursed expenses, making services available, and method of payment are all relevant in this regard. If the worker is making decisions which affect his or her bottom line, the worker likely has the ability to realize profit or loss.

Relationship of the Parties

The relationship of the parties is important because it reflects the parties' intent concerning control. Courts often look to the intent of the parties; this is most often embodied in contractual relationships. A written agreement describing the worker as an independent contractor is viewed as evidence of the party's intent that a worker is an independent contractor—especially in close cases. However, a contractual designation, in and of itself, is not sufficient evidence for determining worker status. The facts and circumstances under which a worker performs services are determinative of a worker's status. This means that the substance of the relationship governs the worker's status, not the label.

Internal Revenue Code §105

Sec. 105. Amounts received under accident and health plans

(a) Amounts attributable to employer contributions

Except as otherwise provided in this section, amounts received by an employee through accident or health insurance for personal injuries or sickness shall be included in gross income to the extent such amounts (1) are attributable to contributions by the employer which were not includible in the gross income of the employee, or (2) are paid by the employer.

(b) Amounts expended for medical care

Except in the case of amounts attributable to (and not in excess of) deductions allowed under section 213 (relating to medical, etc., expenses) for any prior taxable year, gross income does not include amounts referred to in subsection (a) if such amounts are paid, directly or indirectly, to the taxpayer to reimburse the taxpayer for expenses incurred by him for the medical care (as defined in section 213(d)) of the taxpayer, his spouse, and his dependents (as defined in section 152). Any child to whom section 152(e) applies shall be treated as a dependent of both parents for purposes of this subsection.

(c) Payments unrelated to absence from work

Gross income does not include amounts referred to in subsection (a) to the extent such amounts-

(1) constitute payment for the permanent loss or loss of use of a member or function of the body, or the permanent disfigurement, of the taxpayer, his spouse, or a dependent (as defined in section 152), and

(2) are computed with reference to the nature of the injury without regard to the period the employee is absent from work.

(e) Accident and health plans

For purposes of this section and section 104-

(1) amounts received under an accident or health plan for employees, and

(2) amounts received from a sickness and disability fund for employees maintained under the law of a State or the District of Columbia, shall be treated as amounts received through accident or health insurance.

(f) Rules for application of section 213

For purposes of section 213(a) (relating to medical, dental, etc., expenses) amounts excluded from gross income under subsection (c) or (d) shall not be considered as compensation (by insurance or otherwise) for expenses paid for medical care.

(g) Self-employed individual not considered an employee

For purposes of this section, the term "employee" does not include an individual who is an employee within the meaning of section 401(c)(1) (relating to self-employed individuals).

(h) Amount paid to highly compensated individuals under a discriminatory self-insured medical expense reimbursement plan

(1) In general

In the case of amounts paid to a highly compensated individual under a self-insured medical reimbursement plan which does not satisfy the requirements of paragraph (2) for a plan year, subsection (b) shall not apply to such amounts to the extent they constitute an excess reimbursement of such highly compensated individual.

(2) Prohibition of discrimination

A self-insured medical reimbursement plan satisfies the requirements of this paragraph only if-

(A) the plan does not discriminate in favor of highly compensated individuals as to eligibility to participate; and

(B) the benefits provided under the plan do not discriminate in favor of participants who are highly compensated individuals.

(3) Nondiscriminatory eligibility classifications

(A) In general

A self-insured medical reimbursement plan does not satisfy the requirements of subparagraph (A) of paragraph (2) unless such plan benefits-

(i) 70 percent or more of all employees, or 80 percent or more of all the employees who are eligible to benefit under the plan if 70 percent or more of all employees are eligible to benefit under the plan; or

(ii) such employees as qualify under a classification set up by the employer and found by the Secretary not to be discriminatory in favor of highly compensated individuals.

(B) Exclusion of certain employees

For purposes of subparagraph (A), there may be excluded from consideration-

(i) employees who have not completed 3 years of service;

(ii) employees who have not attained age 25;

(iii) part-time or seasonal employees;

(iv) employees not included in the plan who are included in a unit of employees covered by an agreement between employee representatives and one or more employers which the Secretary finds to be a collective bargaining agreement, if accident and health benefits were the subject of good faith bargaining between such employee representatives and such employer or employers; and

(v) employees who are nonresident aliens and who receive no earned income (within the meaning of section 911(d)(2)) from the employer which constitutes income from sources within the United States (within the meaning of section 861(a)(3)).

(4) Nondiscriminatory benefits

A self-insured medical reimbursement plan does not meet the requirements of subparagraph (B) of paragraph (2) unless all benefits provided for participants who are highly compensated individuals are provided for all other participants.

(5) Highly compensated individual defined

For purposes of this subsection, the term "highly compensated individual" means an individual who is

(A) one of the 5 highest paid officers,

(B) a shareholder who owns (with the application of section 318) more than 10 percent in value of the stock of the employer, or

(C) among the highest paid 25 percent of all employees (other than employees described in paragraph (3)(B) who are not participants).

(6) Self-insured medical reimbursement plan

The term "self-insured medical reimbursement plan" means a plan of an employer to reimburse employees for expenses referred to in subsection (b) for which reimbursement is not provided under a policy of accident and health insurance.

(7) Excess reimbursement of highly compensated individual

For purposes of this section, the excess reimbursement of a highly compensated individual which is attributable to a self-insured medical reimbursement plan is-

(A) in the case of a benefit available to highly compensated individuals but not to all other participants (or which otherwise fails to satisfy the requirements of paragraph (2)(B)), the amount reimbursed under the plan to the employee with respect to such benefit, and

(B) in the case of benefits (other than benefits described in subparagraph (A) paid to a highly compensated individual by a plan which fails to satisfy the requirements of paragraph (2), the total amount reimbursed to the highly compensated individual for the plan year multiplied by a fraction-

(i) the numerator of which is the total amount reimbursed to all participants who are highly compensated individuals under the plan for the plan year, and

(ii) the denominator of which is the total amount reimbursed to all employees under the plan for such plan year.

In determining the fraction under subparagraph (B), there shall not be taken into account any reimbursement which is attributable to a benefit described in subparagraph (A).

(8) Certain controlled groups, etc.

All employees who are treated as employed by a single employer under subsection (b), (c), or (m) of section 414 shall be treated as employed by a single employer for purposes of this section.

(9) Regulations

The Secretary shall prescribe such regulations as may be necessary to carry out the provisions of this section.

(10) Time of inclusion

Any amount paid for a plan year that is included in income by reason of this subsection shall be treated as received or accrued in the taxable year of the participant in which the plan year ends.

Treasury Regulations §1.105-11

Sec. 1.105-11 Self-insured medical reimbursement plan.

(a) In general. Under section 105(a), amounts received by an employee through a self-insured medical reimbursement plan which are attributable to contributions of the employer, or are paid by the employer, are included in the employee's gross income unless such amounts are excludable under section 105(b). For amounts reimbursed to a highly compensated individual to be fully excludable from such individual's gross income under section 105(b), the plan must satisfy the requirements of section 105(h) and this section. Section 105(h) is not satisfied if the plan discriminates in favor of highly compensated individuals as to eligibility to participate or benefits. All or a portion of the reimbursements or payments on behalf of such individuals under a discriminatory plan are not excludable from gross income under section 105(b). However, benefits paid to participants who are not highly compensated individuals may be excluded from gross income if the requirements of section 105(b) are satisfied, even if the plan is discriminatory.

(b) Self-insured medical reimbursement plan

(1) General rule

(i) Definition. A self-insured medical reimbursement plan is a separate written plan for the benefit of employees which provides for reimbursement of employee medical expenses referred to in section 105(b). A plan or arrangement is self-insured unless reimbursement is provided under an individual or group policy of accident or health insurance issued by a licensed insurance company or under an arrangement in the nature of a prepaid health care plan that is regulated under federal or state law in a manner similar to the regulation of insurance companies. Thus, for example, a plan of a health maintenance organization, established under the Health Maintenance Organization Act of 1973, would qualify as a prepaid health care plan. In addition, this section applies to a self-insured medical reimbursement plan, determined in accordance with the rules of this section, maintained by an employee organization described in section 501(c)(9).

(ii) Shifting of risk. A plan underwritten by a policy of insurance or a prepaid health care plan that does not involve the shifting of risk to an unrelated third party is considered self-insured for purposes of this section. Accordingly, a cost-plus policy or a policy which in effect merely provides administrative or bookkeeping services is considered self-insured for purposes of this section. However, a plan is not considered self-insured merely because one factor the insurer uses in determining the premium is the employer's prior claims experience.

(iii) Captive insurance company. A plan underwritten by a policy of insurance issued by a captive insurance company is not considered self-insured for purposes of this section if for the plan year the premiums paid by companies unrelated to the captive insurance company equal or exceed 50 percent of the total premiums received and the policy of insurance is similar to policies sold to such unrelated companies.

(2) Other rules. The rules of this section apply to a self-insured portion of an employer's medical plan or arrangement even if the plan is in part underwritten by insurance. For example, if an employer's medical plan reimburses employees for benefits not covered under the insured portion of an overall plan, or for deductible amounts under the insured portions, such reimbursement is subject to the rules of this section. However, a plan which reimburses employees for premiums paid under an insured plan is not subject to this section. In addition, medical expense reimbursements not described in the plan are not paid pursuant to a plan for the benefit of employees, and therefore are not excludable from gross income under section 105(b). Such reimbursements will not affect the determination of whether or not a plan is discriminatory.

(c) Prohibited discrimination

(1) In general. A self-insured medical reimbursement plan does not satisfy the requirements of section 105(h) and this paragraph for a plan year unless the plan satisfies subparagraphs (2) and (3) of this paragraph. However, a plan does not fail to satisfy the requirements of this paragraph merely because benefits under the plan are offset by benefits paid under a self-insured or insured plan of the employer or another employer, or by benefits paid under Medicare or other Federal or State law or similar foreign law. A self-insured plan may take into account the benefits provided under another plan only to the extent that the type of benefit subject to reimbursement is the same under both plans. For example, an amount reimbursed to an employee for a hospital expense under a medical plan maintained by the employer of the employee's spouse may be offset against the self-insured benefit where the self-insured plan covering the employee provides the same type of hospital benefit.

(2) Eligibility to participate

(i) Percentage test. A plan satisfies the requirements of this subparagraph if it benefits—

(A) Seventy percent or more of all employees, or

(B) Eighty percent or more of all the employees who are eligible to benefit under the plan if 70 percent or more of all employees are eligible to benefit under the plan.

(ii) Classification test. A plan satisfies the requirements of this subparagraph if it benefits such employees as qualify under a classification of employees set up by the employer which is found by the Internal Revenue Service not to be discriminatory in favor of highly compensated individuals. In general, this determination will be made based upon the facts and circumstances of each case, applying the same standards as are applied under section 410(b)(1)(B) (relating to qualified pension, profit-sharing and stock bonus plans), without regard to the special rules in section 401(a)(5) concerning eligibility to participate.

(iii) Exclusion of certain employees. Under section 105(h)(3), for purposes of this subparagraph (2), there may be excluded from consideration:

(A) Employees who have not completed 3 years of service prior to the beginning of the plan year. For purposes of this section years of service may be determined by any method that is reasonable and consistent. A determination made in the same manner as (and not requiring service in excess of how) a year of service is determined under section 410(a)(3) shall be deemed to be reasonable. For purposes of the 3-year rule, all of an employee's years of service with the employer prior to a separation from service are not taken into account. For purposes of the 3-year rule, an employee's years of service prior to age 25, as a part-time or seasonal employee, as a member of a collective bargaining unit, or as a nonresident alien, as each is described in this subdivision, are not excluded by reason of being so described from counting towards satisfaction of the rule. In addition, if the employer is a predecessor employer (determined in a manner consistent with section 414(a)), service for such predecessor is treated as service for the employer.

(B) Employees who have not attained age 25 prior to the beginning of the plan year.

(C) Part-time employees whose customary weekly employment is less than 35 hours, if other employees in similar work with the same employer (or, if no employees of the employer are in similar work, in similar work in the same industry and location) have substantially more hours, and seasonal employees whose customary annual employment is less than 9 months, if other employees in similar work with the same employer (or, if no employees of the employer are in similar work, in similar work in the same industry and location) have substantially more months. Notwithstanding the preceding sentence, any employee whose customary weekly employment is less than 25 hours or any employee whose customary annual employment is less than 7 months may be considered as a part-time or seasonal employee.

(D) Employees who are included in a unit of employees covered by an agreement between employee representatives and one or more employers which the Commissioner finds to be a collective bargaining agreement, if accident and health benefits were the subject of good faith bargaining between such employee representatives and such employer or employers. For purposes of determining whether such bargaining occurred, it is not material that such employees are not covered by another medical plan or that the plan was not considered in such bargaining.

(E) Employees who are nonresident aliens and who receive no earned income (within the meaning of section 911(b) and the regulations thereunder) from the employer which constitutes income from sources within the United States (within the meaning of section 861(a)(3) and the regulations thereunder).

(3) Nondiscriminatory benefits

(i) In general. In general, benefits subject to reimbursement under a plan must not discriminate in favor of highly compensated individuals. Plan benefits will not satisfy the requirements of this subparagraph unless all the benefits provided for participants who are highly compensated individuals are provided for all other participants. In addition, all the benefits available for the dependents of employees who are highly compensated individuals must also be available on the same basis for the dependents of all other employees who are participants. A plan that provides optional benefits to participants will be treated as providing a single benefit with respect to the benefits covered by the option provided that (A) all eligible participants may elect any of the benefits covered by the option and (B) there are either no required employee contributions or the required employee contributions are the same amount. This test is applied to the benefits subject to reimbursement under the plan rather than the actual benefit payments or claims under the plan. The presence or absence of such discrimination will be determined by considering the type of benefit subject to reimbursement provided highly compensated individuals, as well as the amount of the benefit subject to reimbursement. A plan may establish a maximum limit for the amount of reimbursement which may be paid a participant for any single benefit, or combination of benefits. However, any maximum limit attributable to employer contributions must be uniform for all participants and for all dependents of employees who are participants and may not be modified by reason of a participant's age or years of service. In addition, if a plan covers employees who are highly compensated individuals, and the type or the amount of benefits subject to reimbursement under the plan are in proportion to employee compensation, the plan discriminates as to benefits.

(ii) Discriminatory operation. Not only must a plan not discriminate on its face in providing benefits in favor of highly compensated individuals, the plan also must not discriminate in favor of such employees in actual operation. The determination of whether plan benefits discriminate in operation in favor of highly compensated individuals is made on the basis of the facts and circumstances of each case. A plan is not considered discriminatory merely because highly compensated individuals participating in the plan utilize a broad range of plan benefits to a greater extent than do other employees participating in the plan. In addition, if a plan (or a particular benefit provided by a plan) is terminated, the termination would cause the plan benefits to be discriminatory if the duration of the plan (or benefit) has the effect of discriminating in favor of highly compensated individuals. Accordingly, the prohibited discrimination may occur where the duration of a particular benefit coincides with the period during which a highly compensated individual utilizes the benefit.

(iii) Retired employees. To the extent that an employer provides benefits under a self-insured medical reimbursement plan to a retired employee that would otherwise be excludible from gross income under section 105(b), determined without regard to section 105(h), such benefits shall not be considered a discriminatory benefit under this paragraph (c). The preceding sentence shall not apply to a retired employee who was a highly compensated individual unless the type, and the dollar limitations, of benefits provided retired employees who were highly compensated individuals are the same for all other retired participants. If this subdivision applies to a retired participant, that individual is not considered an employee for purposes of determining the highest paid 25 percent of all employees under paragraph (d) of this section solely by reason of receiving such plan benefits.

(4) Multiple plans, etc.

(i) General rule. An employer may designate two or more plans as constituting a single plan that is intended to satisfy the requirements of section 105(h)(2) and paragraph (c) of this section, in which case all plans so designated shall be considered as a single plan in determining whether the requirements of such section are satisfied by each of the separate plans. A determination that the combination of plans so designated does not satisfy such requirements does not preclude a determination that one or more of such plans, considered separately, satisfies such requirements. A single plan document may be utilized by an employer for two or more separate plans provided that the employer designates the plans that are to be considered separately and the applicable provisions of each separate plan.

(ii) Other rules. If the designated combined plan discriminates as to eligibility to participate or benefits, the amount of excess reimbursement will be determined under the rules of section 105(h)(7) and paragraph (e) of this section by taking into account all reimbursements made under the combined plan.

(iii) H.M.O. participants. For purposes of section 105(h)(2)(A) and paragraph (c)(2) of this section, a self-insured plan will be deemed to benefit an employee who has enrolled in a health maintenance organization (HMO) that is offered on an optional basis by the employer in lieu of coverage under the self-insured plan if, with respect to that employee, the employer's contributions to the HMO plan equal or exceed those that would be made to the self-insured plan, and if the HMO plan is designated in accordance with subdivision (i) with the self-insured plan as a single plan. For purposes of section 105(h) and this section, except as provided in the preceding sentence, employees covered by, and benefits under, the HMO plan are not treated as part of the self-insured plan.

(d) Highly compensated individuals defined. For purposes of section 105(h) and this section, the term "highly compensated individual" means an individual who is—

(1) One of the 5 highest paid officers,

(2) A shareholder who owns (with the application of section 318) more than 10 percent in value of the stock of the employer, or

(3) Among the highest paid 25 percent of all employees (including the 5 highest paid officers, but not including employees excludable under paragraph (c)(2)(iii) of this section who are not participants in any self-insured medical reimbursement plan of the employer, whether or not designated as a single plan under paragraph (c)(4) of this section, or in a health maintenance organization plan). The status of an employee as an officer or stockholder is determined with respect to a particular benefit on the basis of the employee's officer status or stock ownership at the time during the plan year at which the benefit is provided. In calculating the highest paid 25 percent of all employees, the number of employees included will be rounded to the next highest number. For example, if there are 5 employees, the top two are in the highest paid 25 percent. The level of an employee's compensation is determined on the basis of the employee's compensation for the plan year. For purposes of the preceding sentence, fiscal year plans may determine employee compensation on the basis of the calendar year ending within the plan year.

(e) Excess reimbursement of highly compensated individual

(1) In general. For purposes of section 105(h) and this section, a reimbursement paid to a highly compensated individual is an excess reimbursement if it is paid pursuant to a plan that fails to satisfy the requirements of paragraph (c)(2) or (c)(3) for the plan year. The amount reimbursed to a highly compensated individual which constitutes an excess reimbursement is not excludable from such individual's gross income under section 105(b).

(2) Discriminatory benefit. In the case of a benefit available to highly compensated individuals but not to all other participants (or which otherwise discriminates in favor of highly compensated individuals as opposed to other participants), the amount of excess reimbursement equals the total amount reimbursed to the highly compensated individual with respect to the benefit.

(3) Discriminatory coverage. In the case of benefits (other than discriminatory benefits described in subparagraph (2)) paid to a highly compensated individual under a plan which fails to satisfy the requirements of paragraph (c)(2) relating to nondiscrimination in eligibility to participate, the amount of excess reimbursement is determined by multiplying the total amount reimbursed to the individual by a fraction. The numerator of the fraction is the total amount reimbursed during that plan year to all highly compensated individuals. The denominator of the fraction is the total amount reimbursed during that plan year to all participants. In computing the fraction and the total amount reimbursed to the individual, discriminatory benefits described in subparagraph (2) are not taken into account. Accordingly, any amount which is included in income by reason of the benefit's not being available to all other participants will not be taken into account.

(4) Examples. The provisions of this paragraph are illustrated by the following examples:

Example (1). Corporation M maintains a self-insured medical reimbursement plan which covers all employees. The plan provides the following maximum limits on the amount of benefits subject to reimbursement: $5,000 for officers and $1,000 for all other participants. During a plan year Employee A, one of the 5 highest paid officers, received reimbursements in the amount of $4,000. Because the amount of benefits provided for highly compensated individuals is not provided for all other participants, the plan benefits are discriminatory. Accordingly, Employee A received an excess reimbursement of $3,000 ($4,000-$1,000) which constitutes a benefit available to highly compensated individuals, but not to all other participants.

Example (2). Corporation N maintains a self-insured medical reimbursement plan which covers all employees. The plan provides a broad range of medical benefits subject to reimbursement for all participants. However, only the 5 highest paid officers are entitled to dental benefits. During the plan year Employee B, one of the 5 highest paid officers, received dental payments under the plan in the amount of $300. Because dental benefits are provided for highly compensated individuals, and not for all other participants, the plan discriminates as to benefits. Accordingly, Employee B received an excess reimbursement in the amount of $300.

Example (3). Corporation O maintains a self-insured medical reimbursement plan which discriminates as to eligibility by covering only the highest paid 40% of all employees. Benefits subject to reimbursement under the plan are the same for all participants. During a plan year Employee C, a highly compensated individual, received benefits in the amount of $1,000. The amount of excess reimbursement paid Employee C during the plan year will be calculated by multiplying the $1,000 by a fraction determined under subparagraph (3).

Example (4). Corporation P maintains a self-insured medical reimbursement plan for its employees. Benefits subject to reimbursement under the plan are the same for all plan participants. However, the plan fails the eligibility tests of section 105(h)(3)(A) and thereby discriminates as to eligibility. During the 1980 plan year Employee D, a highly compensated individual, was hospitalized for surgery and incurred medical expenses of $4,500 which were reimbursed to D under the plan. During that plan year the Corporation P medical plan paid $50,000 in benefits under the plan, $30,000 of which constituted benefits paid to highly compensated individuals. The amount of excess reimbursement not excludable by D under section 105(b) is $2,700 ($4500 x $30,000/$50,000)

Example (5). Corporation Q maintains a self-insured medical reimbursement plan for its employees. The plan provides a broad range of medical benefits subject to reimbursement for participants. However, only the five highest paid officers are entitled to dental benefits. In addition, the plan fails the eligibility test of section 105(h)(3)(A) and thereby discriminates as to eligibility. During the calendar 1981 plan year, Employee E, a highly compensated individual, received dental benefits under the plan in the amount of $300, and no other employee received dental benefits. In addition, Employee E was hospitalized for surgery and incurred medical expenses, reimbursement for which was available to all participants, of $4,500 which were reimbursed to E under the plan. Because dental benefits are only provided for highly compensated individuals, Employee E received an excess reimbursement under paragraph (e)(2) above in the amount of $300. For the 1981 plan year, the Corporation Q medical plan paid $50,300 in total benefits under the plan, $30,300 of which constituted benefits paid to highly compensated individuals. In computing the fraction under paragraph (e)(3), discriminatory benefits described in paragraph (e)(2) are not taken into account. Therefore, the amount of excess reimbursement not excludable to Employee E with respect to the $4,500 of medical expenses incurred is $2,700 ($4,500 x $30,000/$50,000) and the total amount of excess reimbursements includable in E's income for 1981 is $3,000.

Example (6) Corporation R maintains a calendar year self-insured medical reimbursement plan which covers all employees. The type of benefits subject to reimbursement under the plan include all medical care expenses as defined in section 213(e). The amount of reimbursement available to any employee for any calendar year is limited to 5 percent of the compensation paid to each employee during the calendar year. The amount of compensation and reimbursement paid to Employees A-F for the calendar year is as follows:

Employee	Compensation	Reimbursable amount paid
A.....................................	$100,000	$5,000
B.....................................	25,000	1,250
C.....................................	15,000	750
D.....................................	10,000	500
E.....................................	10,000	500
F.....................................	8,000	400
		8,400

(ii) Because the amount of benefits subject to reimbursement under the plan is in proportion to employee compensation the plan discriminates as to benefits. In addition, Employees A and B are highly compensated individuals. The amount of excess reimbursement paid Employees A and B during the plan year will be determined under paragraph (e)(2). Because benefits in excess of $400 (Employee F's maximum benefit) are provided for highly compensated individuals and not for all other participants, Employees A and B received, respectively, an excess reimbursement of $4,600 and $850.

(f) Certain controlled groups. For purposes of applying the provisions of section 105(h) and this section, all employees who are treated as employed by a single employer under section 414 (b) and (c), and the regulations thereunder (relating to special rules for qualified pension, profit-sharing and stock bonus plans), shall be treated as employed by a single employer.

(g) Exception for medical diagnostic procedures

(1) In general. For purposes of applying section 105(h) and this section, reimbursements paid under a plan for medical diagnostic procedures for an employee, but not a dependent, are not considered to be a part of a plan described in this section. The medical diagnostic procedures include routine medical examinations, blood tests, and X-rays. Such procedures do not include expenses incurred for the treatment, cure or testing of a known illness or disability, or treatment or testing for a physical injury, complaint or specific symptom of a bodily malfunction. For example, a routine dental examination with X-rays is a medical diagnostic procedure, but X-rays and treatment for a specific complaint are not. In addition, such procedures do not include any activity undertaken for exercise, fitness, nutrition, recreation, or the general improvement of health unless they are for medical care as defined in section 213(e). The diagnostic procedures must be performed at a facility which provides no services (directly or indirectly) other than medical, and ancillary, services. For purposes of the preceding sentence, physical proximity between a medical facility and nonmedical facilities will not for that reason alone cause the medical facility not to qualify. For example, an employee's annual physical examination conducted at the employee's personal physician's office is not considered a part of the medical reimbursement plan and therefore is not subject to the nondiscrimination requirements. Accordingly, the amount reimbursed may be excludable from the employee's income if the requirements of section 105(b) are satisfied.

(2) Transportation, etc. expenses. Transportation expenses primarily for an allowable diagnostic procedure are included within the exception described in this paragraph, but only to the extent they are ordinary and necessary. Transportation undertaken merely for the general improvement of health, or in connection with a vacation, is not within the scope of this exception, nor are any incidental expenses for food or lodging; therefore, amounts reimbursed for such expenses may be excess reimbursements under paragraph (e).

(h) Time of inclusion. Excess reimbursements (determined under paragraph (e)) paid to a highly compensated individual for a plan year will be considered as received in the taxable year of the individual in which (or with which) the plan year ends. The particular plan year to which reimbursements relate shall be determined under the plan provisions. In the absence of plan provisions reimbursements shall be attributed to the plan year in which payment is made. For example, under a calendar year plan an excess reimbursement paid to A in 1981 on account of an expense incurred and subject to reimbursement for the 1980 plan year under the terms of the plan will be considered as received in 1980 by A.

(i) Self-insured contributory plan. A medical plan subject to this section may provide for employer and employee contributions. See Sec. 1.105-1(c). The tax treatment of reimbursements attributable to employee contributions is determined under section 104(a)(3). The tax treatment of reimbursements attributable to employer contributions is determined under section 105. The amount of reimbursements which are attributable to contributions of the employer shall be determined in accordance with Sec. 1.105-1(e).

(j) Effective date. Section 105(h) and this section are effective for taxable years beginning after December 31, 1979 and for amounts reimbursed after December 31, 1979. In determining plan discrimination and the taxability of excess reimbursements made for a plan year beginning in 1979 and ending in 1980, a plan's eligibility and benefit requirements as well as actual reimbursements made in the plan year during 1979, will not be taken into account. In addition, this section does not apply to expenses which are incurred in 1979 and paid in 1980.

(k) Special rules

(1) Relation to cafeteria plans. If a self-insured medical reimbursement plan is included in a cafeteria plan as described in section 125, the rules of this section will determine the status of a benefit as a taxable or nontaxable benefit, and the rules of section 125 will determine whether an employee is taxed as though he elected all available taxable benefits (including taxable benefits under a discriminatory medical reimbursement plan). This rule is illustrated by the following example:

Example. Corporation M maintains a cafeteria plan described in section 125. Under the plan an officer of the corporation may elect to receive medical benefits provided by a self-insured medical reimbursement plan which is subject to the rules of this section. However, the self-insured medical reimbursement plan fails the nondiscrimination rules under paragraph (c) of this section. Accordingly, the amount of excess reimbursement is taxable to the officer participating in the medical reimbursement plan pursuant to section 105(h) and this section. Therefore, the self-insured medical reimbursement plan will be considered a taxable benefit under section 125 and the regulations thereunder.

(2) Benefit subject to reimbursement. For purposes of this section, a benefit subject to reimbursement is a benefit described in the plan under which a claim for reimbursement or for a payment directly to the health service provider may be

filed by a plan participant. It does not refer to actual claims or benefit reimbursements paid under a plan.

0-595-34243-4

www.ingramcontent.com/pod-product-compliance
Lightning Source LLC
Chambersburg PA
CBHW021040180526
45163CB00005B/2203